COMMUNITY CARE: AGENDA FOR ACTION

A REPORT TO THE SECRETARY OF STATE FOR SOCIAL SERVICES BY SIR ROY GRIFFITHS

LONDON

HER MAJESTY'S STATIONERY OFFICE

ISBN 0 11 321130 9

Dear Secretary of State,

1. In December 1986 your predecessor, Mr Norman Fowler, asked me to undertake an overview of community care policy. The emphasis was specifically that the review should be brief and geared towards advice on action as was the review of management in the health service in 1983.

2. The precise terms of reference were – "To review the way in which public funds are used to support community care policy and to advise me on the options for action that would improve the use of these funds as a contribution to more effective community care".

3. The review is accordingly brief as requested. The recommendations are summarised immediately following this introduction and the main text explains the proposals in more detail. I regard them as essentially the first stages in a flow chart. If they are acceptable in principle, then there is considerable further work to be done by way of analysis of responsibilities, funding mechanisms, etc.. If they are unacceptable, then the brevity will have been even more appropriate.

4. It was particularly emphasised that the inquiry should not be a Royal Commission type investigation taking formal evidence. Indeed the Audit Commission report (December 1986) 'Making a Reality of Community Care' and the report of The House of Commons Social Services Committee on "Community Care with special reference to adult mentally ill and mentally handicapped people" (HC 13 1984–85) to a great extent made this unnecessary. These two reports contain the essential facts on which this review is based.

5. Nevertheless whilst not asking for formal evidence I have received a large number of submissions and have supplemented these by extensive discussions and visits. There is in addition a formidably voluminous body of other literature. Many submissions have been received on a whole range of detailed points. Where they are relevant to the main thrust of the review they have been reflected in the general conclusions. In all other cases they have been noted separately for consideration.

6. Some of the submissions recommended changes in the content of policy. I have not regarded this as within my brief except in one or two rare instances; my work is essentially geared to ensuring that the machinery and resources exist to implement such policies as are determined.

7. Many of the submissions have drawn attention to inadequacies of funding. Again my remit is not to deal with the level of funding but rather to suggest how resources, whatever the level, may better be directed. The Audit Commission on the one hand were satisfied that better value could be obtained from existing resources. On the other hand many social services departments and voluntary groups grappling with the problems at local level certainly felt that the Israelites faced with the requirement to make bricks without straw had a comparatively routine and possible task.

8. Equally the review is not about cost reduction. Cost improvement, by which I mean the more efficient use of resources, is at the heart of any management process and should be characteristic of the use of whatever money is available. But emphatically I have not been asked to provide recommendations aimed at reducing the total levels of expenditure, whether in the health service, the social services departments or elsewhere.

9. There is a temptation against the background of the Audit Commission's work to tackle at the outset the matters highlighted, of funding on the one hand and, on the other, the complex network of relationships and responsibilities at the local level between the various authorities, voluntary groups, etc.. I chose first to view the position at the two extremes, of policy at the centre and consumer satisfaction in the field. At the centre, community care has been talked of for thirty years and in few areas can the gap between political rhetoric and policy on the one hand, or between policy and reality in the field on the other hand have been so great. To talk of policy in matters of care except in the context of available resources and timescales for action owes more to theology than to the purposeful delivery of a caring service. This is not an argument in itself for more resources: the imperative is that policy and resources should come into reasonable relationship, so that we are clear about what community care services are trying to achieve and so that leadership and direction to those providing service can be given. The problem is compounded by the responsibility for inputs to community care at the centre being divided between the two arms of the DHSS, the Social Security and the Health and Personal Social Services sides, and the Department of the Environment – a feeling that community care is a poor relation; everybody's distant relative but nobody's baby.

10. At the other extreme one is immediately struck by differences between the arrangements for provision of medical and non-medical care. If a person is in need of medical care he knows that he has to contact his GP, who will then arrange for appropriate medical care to be given. It would be too elaborate and indeed inappropriate for a similar system to be set up for non-medical care. What is surprising however is that such a system involving the assignment of a person in need of support to an individual carer, so as to become his responsibility, is rarely made, even where it would be highly applicable, e.g. in the case of patients discharged from long stay hospitals.

11. If we are clear what we are trying to do by way of Government policy and if we can build up what is required at local level from knowledge and assessment of individual need, then we can move on to look at the machinery and structure to deliver this – or rather to allow it to be delivered. The aim must be to provide structure and resources to support the initiatives, the innovation and the commitment at local level and to allow them to flourish; to encourage the success stories in one area to become the commonplace of achievement everywhere else. To prescribe from the centre will be to shrivel the varied pattern of local activity.

12. The first approach on structure must be to see why at present care is not being delivered effectively. Major restructuring can be disruptive and time-consuming and before it is contemplated it has to be shown that the existing authorities are incapable of delivering; in short, we have to be satisfied that it is not the roadblocks to achievement which are the major problems, but the vehicles themselves.

13. We are equally left with the problem that no matter how much we restructure we simply move the interface between responsible authorities. Collaboration is vital, whether in planning, financing or implementation. The history of joint planning or financing is far from reassuring, but again can it be made to work in default of major restructuring, possibly by incentives and sanctions?

14. I have referred to roadblocks. The system for the distribution of rate support grant makes it extremely difficult for local authorities to commit themselves confidently to collaboration with the health authorities. This has been recognised by Government with the introduction of measures such as joint finance for the direct transfer of funds, but the problems highlighted by the Audit Commission remain, along with the related problems of the inadequacy of bridging finance.

15. The Audit Commission highlighted the policy conflicts and perverse incentives which exist in the impact of supplementary benefit payments for residential care on community care policies. This particular benefit is at the interface between the social security open-ended financial commitment based on entitlement and a budgeted provision against priority of need, which is the social services approach. Prima facie the two approaches are diametrically opposed.

16. The present provision of social security for residential care is not wholly bad; the unintentional consequence of Government action has been to provide accommodation for large numbers of people, many of whom would have needed it and by international comparisons we do not as yet have excessive numbers of people in residential accommodation. The arguments against it are that the ready availability of social security makes it easy to provide residential accommodation for an individual regardless of whether it is in his best interest. Secondly if overall resources are limited residential accommodation may take an undue proportion of available money to the exclusion of more satisfactory alternatives of keeping people in their own homes. To use an increasingly expensive social security provision as a safety valve to keep the lid on the pot of community provision would be inconsistent with governmental and managerial responsibility.

17. If a solution is found to this question one is left with the further anomaly exposed that it is a matter of chance whether a person needing long stay care finds himself in a geriatric ward, or in a nursing home or a residential home, with different costs and charging. Certainly a common approach is needed.

18. Dominant in discussions and visits was the question of the closure of the large mental hospitals. Representations ranged inevitably around the desirability of the policy and problems of implementation. The policy and its implementation are matters of major national importance and need to be recognised and handled as such. Each closure needs approval, monitoring and control at the highest level. No person should be discharged without a clear package of care devised and without being the responsibility of a named care worker. This is not simply an administrative or financial process: it is intended to be a thorough process of review to guarantee that there are carefully prepared plans to ensure an optimal quality of life for the individuals leaving hospital – plans which are above all realistic in the light of the particular community and of the staffing and facilities likely to be available.

19. Overall the submissions ranged from minor departures from the status quo to a exhortation to seek radical solutions. As to the status quo, the Audit Commission warned that the one option that is not tenable is to do nothing; the history of piecemeal changes compounding the confusion in community care suggests that I am thus debarred from what might otherwise have been the safest option.

20. At the other extreme the urging to be radical has generally implied that I should tear up the present organisational structures and start afresh. I have decided to be even more radical. Nothing could be more radical in the public sector than to spell out responsibilities, insist on performance and accountability and to evidence that action is being taken; and even more radical, to match policy with appropriate resources and agreed timescales. I emphasise responsibilities; collaboration, joint planning, joint finance are admirable provided that in the first place responsibilities are clear and, in the absence of collaboration, authorities can be held accountable. Of course this would be helped by restructuring at the local level with health authorities, social services authorities and family practitioner committees enjoying co-terminosity, or even being brought within a common structure. To make restructuring mandatory would be enormously distruptive and would create turmoil under a semblance of action. I believe that there is a diversity of response at local level which is appropriate and would be forthcoming in the planning system proposed. Some clarification has inevitably, however difficult the task, to be sought between the role of health authorities and social services authorities.

21. The recommendations are detailed at the end of this introduction. There are a number of keystones.

22. At the centre a new focus for community care should be provided with a Minister clearly and publicly identified as responsible for community care. Funding of social services authorities should be by way of specific grant amounting to say 50 per cent of the costs of an approved programme (with an upper limit on the grant but not necessarily on total expenditure). Alternatively the grant might be slightly lower (say 40 per cent – 45 per cent) to indicate that the primary responsibility for community care should correctly lie with the Local Authority. The composition of the fund is detailed in the report. Approval of the social services authority's programme is simply designed to ensure that plans are well thought through; that they represent value for money at local level and meet the needs of the locality; that adequate provision is being made for support of the voluntary groups and that they are participating in the preparation and implementation of the plan; that the role of the informal carer is appropriately supported; and finally and importantly that the commitment and contribution of the appropriate housing and health authorities have been secured as part of the plan.

23. In short there must be a clear framework within which local and health authorities are working out their own process of co-ordination. The programme should be matched by parallel approval of those parts of the health service plans allocated and ring-fenced for community care. Approval of the health service allocation should normally, of course, be part of the health service review process. As far as possible however it is desirable that the plans of the health service and social services, with support of the local voluntary groups, should together be

submitted and should evidence the appropriate collaborative framework. The only exception to this general approval would be for certain major programmes of national importance e.g. closure of long-stay hospitals where resources would be targeted to ensure implementation against much more detailed plans.

24. At local level the role of social services authoritites should be reorientated towards ensuring that the needs of individuals within the specified groups are identified, packages of care are devised and services co-ordinated; and where appropriate a specific care manager is assigned. The type of services to be provided would be derived from analysis of the individual care needs: the responsibility of the social services authorities is to ensure that these services are provided within the appropriate budgets by the public or private sector according to where they can be provided most economically and efficiently. The onus in all cases should be on the social services authorities to show that the private sector is being fully stimulated and encouraged and that competitive tenders or other means of testing the market, are being taken.

25. This is a key statement. The role of the public sector is essentially to ensure that care is provided. How it is provided is an important, but secondary consideration and local authorities must show that they are getting and providing real value.

26. As to residential accommodation social services authorities would be responsible for assessing whether a move to such accommodation was in the best interests of the individual and what the local authority would be prepared to pay for. This would be achieved by the social security benefit for residential accommodation being limited to a fixed maximum sum, substantially lower than at present, payable on the present basis with the rest being paid by the social services authority against an assessment of need for care. The alternative is to leave the entitlement as it is, payable in total by social security, but to make it payable only against an assessment by the social services authority and to have part of the social security allowance recharged to the social services authority, either immediately or by way of subtraction from the central specific grant. As part of the decision making process the social services authority should take account of the total resources available for the provision of care. The aim would be first, to preserve entitlements whilst putting the social services authority in a position of financial neutrality in deciding what form of care would be in the best interests of the individual and secondly to ensure that individuals are not placed in residential accommodation, when it is not in their best interests.

27. I believe that the above will provide an acceptable framework. It substitutes for the discredited refuge of imploring collaboration and exhorting action a new requirement that collaboration and action are present normally as a condition for grant. It places responsibility for care clearly within the local community, which – subject to minimum provisions for all sections of the disadvantaged groups – can best determine where money should be spent. It will bolster experiment and innovation at local level by not being prescriptive about organisation. The recommendations as to the changed role for social services authorites were foreshadowed by the Barclay Report in 1983. The essence of the present proposals is that there is machinery to ensure that it happens.

28. But any recommendations are made with a full appreciation that implementation will bring problems. There is no neat perfect solution waiting to be discovered –

no Rubik Cube which will be perfectly solved if one can get the various components appropriately related. The reality is that one is faced, whether in making recommendations or in their implementation, with a choice between unsatisfactory alternatives. In many areas, in addition to responsibilities needing to be defined more precisely and management structures to be effectively established, there is a particular need to collect data in order to permit decisions as to the cost-effective use of resources. The present lack of refined information systems and management accounting within any of the authorities to whom one might look centrally or locally to be responsible for community care would plunge most organisations in the private sector into a quick and merciful liquidation. This has in any case to be remedied in the interests of an effective service and I am confident that the social services authorities will meet this particular challenge.

29. The proposals face up to what may be regarded as a danger by some local authorities that there will be more central control of community care. The control is actually intended to be a minimum consistent with there being any national policy in this area and is designed simply to ensure and evidence at local level that the matter is being taken seriously and that the framework of collaborative care is established and working; in exceptional cases, such as the closure of major mental hospitals, a much more detailed plan would be required. Any less control is inconsistent with the claim that there is a national policy.

30. At the same time the proposals are designed to ensure that the real responsibility for seeing that appropriate care is provided is at local level with the social services authorities and the health authorities. If community care means anything, it is that responsibility is placed as near to the individual and his carers as possible. I also believe that where the priorities between different groups may differ widely according to local needs, the right and indeed obligation to determine that should be as local as possible and with the locally elected authority. It cannot be managed in detail from Whitehall, but it has to be managed.

31. The move to specific grant is important. It should be seen as liberating to local authorities to have more certainty. It will provide an instrument of central control, but it should not be seen as an instrument of constraint.

32. Because of the importance of the Audit Commission report, many of the submissions which I received fastened on the Commission's recommendations for consideration of a lead authority for the mentally ill, and the elderly and the mentally and physically handicapped respectively. I have side-stepped these recommendations, largely because I believe that the starting point has to be to identify and respond reasonably and appropriately to the needs of individuals in their particular circumstances. How these needs are to be met will call for particular responses, one of which in a given locality may be to provide special facilities for the elderly or the handicapped and to organise accordingly. The emphasis, however, is that the structures have to be responsive to the local situation and there is room for infinite experiment.

33. The recommendations do not preclude the establishment of lead authorities by agreement at local level, submitted for approval to the centre as part of the local plan. This could extend to the lead authority being given the funds and being the paymaster by buying back services from wherever necessary. To make this

concept of lead authority mandatory however would, I believe, be premature and over-prescriptive at this stage.

34. I also received submissions on staffing and training and unresolved issues on terms and conditions for staff. An overriding impression on training is the insularity of training for each professional group. It may be over ambitious to talk about common training in skills for everyone working in the community, but an understanding by each profession about the role of the other professions in the community could easily be achieved. Again this type of collaboration at local level in training matters should form part of the basic plan.

35. There may in fact be a tendency to over elaborate, both as to the professional input and the training required. Many of the needs of elderly and disabled people are for help of a practical nature (getting dressed, shopping, cleaning). There is need for a new multi-purpose auxiliary force to be given limited training and to give help of a practical nature in the field of community care. There is little likelihood that the professions will be available in the numbers required to cover all aspects of community care, but more importantly it is a waste of resources to be leaving this type of practical work to them. Certainly major experiments should be initiated and should involve not only mature adults, but particularly school leavers, YTS etc.. To some extent this is already being tried with an extension of the role of home helps in certain authorities.

36. On terms and conditions for staff transferred between authorities as a result of the move to community care, a variety of solutions are possible. What is inexcusable is the inordinate delay in setting out these solutions for the transfer of staff. The alternatives are mentioned in the report and a clear decision should be given.

37. The main body of the report deals with the transitional provisions at local level; the aim would be to minimise disruption and essentially to provide a framework which will encourage and facilitate achievements which are present in many areas today despite the system.

38. The general banner under which many submissions were made carried the legend "Care in the community is not a cheap option". It is worth reiterating that I was not asked to consider the level of resources appropriate. I have, however, insisted that we should be quite open as to what we are seeking to achieve and be realistic as to what policies can be pursued with the likely available money. What cannot be acceptable is to allow ambitious policies to be embarked on without the appropriate funds. On many counts poorly implemented programmes for change are very often worse than the status quo. Even with the improved machinery of handling and funding which are recommended, if we try to pursue unrealistic policies the resources will be spread transparently thin.

39. I believe that the recommendations contained in this review should answer most of the points made by the Audit Commission, but I have the occasional sinking feeling that there is nothing so outdated as to provide today's solution to today's problem. It is however a necessary preliminary to thinking ahead and a precaution to ensuring that nothing is recommended which is inconsistent with tomorrow's scene. There is a need to experiment with a whole variety of initiatives –

social/health maintenance organisations, insurance/tax incentives, not simply for the individual, but for the individual in a family context. Tomorrow's thinking in corporate personnel departments on provision and assurance for community care requirements may be the equivalent of the corporate pension thinking of thirty years ago, with the same opportunities for care to be provided as a result of employer/employee contributions into a corporate scheme. More immediately there is no reason why, on a controlled basis, social services authorities should not experiment with vouchers or credits for particular levels of community care, allowing individuals to spend them on particular forms of domiciliary care and to choose between particular suppliers as they wish.

40. I have made suggestions as to the next stages of work and implementation. I believe the recommendations contain the best blend of purpose, practicality and minimum disruption and provide an appropriate base for a much improved delivery of community care.

41. May I finally thank first my support team from the Department – Martin Woolley, Nicholas Bromley, Chris Kenny, Linda Barnard and Frances Graham – for their unremitting efforts over the past twelve months, and the team of outside Advisers who have guided me throughout and contributed extensively to the thinking behind the Report. Whilst the recommendations are my own, I am grateful to the Advisers for indicating that they are supportive both of the style and content of the report.

12 February 1988

COMMUNITY CARE: AGENDA FOR ACTION

Contents

Chapter 1: Summary of Proposals for Action

1.1 I recommend that the following steps be taken to create better opportunities for the successful and efficient delivery of community care policies for adults who are mentally ill, mentally handicapped, elderly or physically disabled and similar groups.

1.2 Central government should ensure that there is a Minister of State in DHSS, seen by the public as being clearly responsible for community care. His role should be strengthened and clarified in the light of the other recommendations. His responsibilities would include:

1.2.1 preparing and publishing a clear, short, statement of government's community care objectives and priorities;

1.2.2 deciding on those areas in which government wishes to lay down standards of service delivery;

1.2.3 making arrangements for reviewing local social services authority plans, against national objectives, and for linking that process with the allocation of resources;

1.2.4 setting up adequate machinery for identifying the results of local social services authority activity;

1.2.5 making arrangements for the distribution of the specific grant recommended below, and ensuring the necessary matching between policy objectives and the resources provided to meet them;

1.2.6 ensuring through the NHS planning and review machinery that community care objectives are adequately reflected in health authority plans and the allocation of resources to health authorities.

1.3 Local social services authorities should, within the resources available:

1.3.1 assess the community care needs of their locality, set local priorities and service objectives, and develop local plans in consultation with health authorities in particular (but also others including housing authorities, voluntary bodies, and private providers of care) for delivering those objectives;

1.3.2 identify and assess individuals' needs, taking full account of personal preferences (and those of informal carers), and design packages of care best suited to enabling the consumer to live as normal a life as possible;

1.3.3 arrange the delivery of packages of care to individuals, building first on the available contribution of informal carers and neighbourhood support, then the provision of domiciliary and day services or, if appropriate, residential care;

1.3.4 act for these purposes as the designers, organisers and purchasers of non-health care services, and not primarily as direct providers, making the maximum possible use of voluntary and private sector bodies to widen consumer choice, stimulate innovation and encourage efficiency.

1.4 To enable this to happen, local social services authorities must be put into a position to take a more comprehensive view of care needs and services. Therefore they should be made responsible for:

1.4.1 assessing the need for residential care and, if they judge it appropriate, meeting the costs of caring for people who cannot pay for themselves, in residential (including nursing) homes above a basic level of support. (This basic support should continue to be available as a social security entitlement, at a level broadly in line with that available to people in the community.);

1.4.2 funding the community care projects currently supported through the NHS resources described as "Joint Finance";

1.4.3 spending the money currently allocated to the community care grant elements of the Social Fund, with discretion to decide on what goods and services should be provided.

These changes will release local social service authorities from pressures, which can distort the delivery of publicly supported services.

1.5 Equally to enable action to be taken, local social services authorities will need confidence that their resources can match their responsibilities. Therefore:

1.5.1 central government should arrange for the necessary transfer of resources between central and local government to match the defined responsibilities;

1.5.2 in order to provide the necessary basis for planning, create the desired relationship between central and local government in the delivery of policies, and ensure that resources are used for their intended purposes, social services authorities should be supported by general and targeted specific grants providing a significant proportion of the total cost of the programme;

1.5.3 payment of specific grant should be conditional on central government being satisfied that local social services authorities have adequate management systems, including planning machinery in place; and that local objectives are sufficiently in line with government policy.

1.6 It is further recommended that:

1.6.1 health authorities should continue to be responsible for medically required community health services, including making any necessary input into assessing needs and delivering packages of care;

1.6.2 general medical practitioners should be responsible for ensuring that local social services authorities are aware of their patients' needs for non-health care;

1.6.3 public housing authorities should be responsible for providing and financing only the "bricks and mortar" of housing for community care;

1.6.4 authorities should have the power to act jointly, or as agents for each other;

1.6.5 distribution of specific grant should take account of the extent to which consumers in a local authority area are able to meet the full economic cost of services;

1.6.6 the functions of a "community carer" should be developed into a new occupation, with appropriate training, so that one person can, as far as possible, provide whatever personal and practical assistance an individual requires.

1.7 To manage implementation, I recommend that:

1.7.1 the Minister be responsible for developing the necessary action plans, including those that will require legislation, and supervising their implementation;

1.7.2 the Minister be supported by an implementation team.

1.7.3 the training implications of my recommendations be assessed.

Chapter 2: Background and General Approach

2.1 I was asked by the then Secretary of State for Social Services, Mr Norman Fowler, to undertake an overview of community care policy on 16 December 1986. The formal terms of reference were:—

"To review the way in which public funds are used to support community care policy and to advise me on options which would improve the use of these funds as a contribution to more effective community care."

I was asked to gear my recommendations towards advice on action, and have done so in Chapter 1.

2.2 This chapter describes my general approach to the task, and method of working.

Interpretation of Terms of Reference

2.3 The review has concentrated on adults who require more than the usual care and support from others because they are elderly, mentally ill, mentally handicapped, or physically disabled. I have taken community care to be care and support for these and similar groups.

2.4 I was not asked to consider child care issues. A similar approach to that which is recommended may however be relevant in that context.

2.5 The review encompasses the roles of families and friends (the so-called informal carers); volunteers and the organised voluntary sector; private profit-making services; and public services in the provision of community care. The report concentrates on the action needed in the fields of personal social services, health services and social security. I have not felt precluded from considering the contribution of other public services such as housing, education and transport, but have not found it necessary to make extensive recommendations in those areas.

2.6 I have reviewed the full range of services which make up community care: those provided to people in their own homes, group homes, residential care homes, hostels and nursing homes. I have not therefore considered hospital in-patients, who require both medical supervision and twenty-four hour availability of nursing support.

2.7 The recommendations for health and personal social services are directed to the position in England. Social security is administered on a common basis throughout Great Britain and on a fully parallel basis in Northern Ireland. The recommendations about social security in particular have implications for services in Scotland, Wales and Northern Ireland which will need further consideration.

Method of Approach

2.8 The Audit Commission Report "Making a Reality of Community Care" (published in December 1986) provided a valuable description and analysis of current problems. Other publications have since made helpful contributions to the debate including "Public Support for Residential Care" (the Report of the Joint Central and Local Government Working Party), "Community Care Developments" by the National Audit Office, and an Audit Commission Occasional Paper "Community Care: Developing Services for People with a Mental Handicap". I have had helpful contact with the Independent Review of Residential Care, chaired by Lady Wagner, which has been working throughout the period in which I have been conducting my review.

2.9 I have not seen my primary task as one of fact finding. The facts have already been well documented in the publications I have described, and the issues have been well identified. My job has been to produce proposals for action, and the report sets out not to add to the volume of information about community care, but to explain the proposals.

2.10 By visits, extensive discussions and through the written material sent to me, I have learned the views of consumers and front line providers of community care, as well as those of managers and policy makers. I am grateful to all those who have shared their knowledge and views with me.

2.11 I have been greatly helped by a panel of Advisers, who throughout have given me unstintingly the benefit of their knowledge and experience as I developed my proposals. They are:

Dorothy Blenkinsop, Regional Nursing Officer, Northern Regional Health Authority;

Dr Peter Horrocks, formerly Director of the Health Advisory Service and currently Consultant Physician (Priority Services Development), Yorkshire Regional Health Authority;

Geoffrey Hulme, Director of the Public Expenditure Policy Unit;

Ken Judge, Director of the King's Fund Institute;

John Kay, Director of the Centre for Business Strategy and Professor in Industrial Policy, London Business School;

Herbert Laming, Director of Social Services, Hertfordshire;

Jill Pitkeathley, Director of the National Council for Carers and their Elderly Dependants; and

Sir James Swaffield, former Director General of the Greater London Council.

I am grateful for all the help I have been given, although the recommendations are entirely my own responsibility.

Chapter 3: Community Care

What is Community Care?

3.1 This chapter sets out the approach to the value and purpose of community care and the role of the State in its provision.

The Role of the State

3.2 Publicly provided services constitute only a small part of the total care provided to people in need. Families, friends, neighbours and other local people provide the majority of care in response to needs which they are uniquely well placed to identify and respond to. This will continue to be the primary means by which people are enabled to live normal lives in community settings. The proposals take as their starting point that this is as it should be, and that the first task of publicly provided services is to support and where possible strengthen these networks of carers. Public services can help by identifying such actual and potential carers, consulting them about their needs and those of the people they are caring for, and tailoring the provision of extra services (if required) accordingly.

3.3 The second task of the publicly provided services is to identify where these caring networks have broken down, or cannot meet the needs, and decide what public services are desirable to fill the gap.

3.4 The primary function of the public services is to design and arrange the provision of care and support in line with people's needs. That care and support can be provided from a variety of sources. There is value in a multiplicity of provision, not least from the consumer's point of view, because of the widening of choice, flexibility, innovation and competition it should stimulate. The proposals are therefore aimed at stimulating the further development of the "mixed economy" of care. It is vital that social services authorities should see themselves as the arrangers and purchasers of care services – not as monopolistic providers.

3.5 The resources available for public services will always be finite. As well as assessing needs and arranging suitable services, managers of public services are therefore bound to apply priorities. A fundamental purpose of the proposals is to ensure that someone is in a position to apply priorities in a way that maximises the chances that those most in need will receive due care, and that eliminates the possibility of low priority need being met while higher priorities are neglected.

Value and Purpose of Community Care

3.6 Much of the comment I have received during the review urged me to make recommendations about specific services. It is first important to identify the principles and objectives of community care which can then be used to guide the development of appropriate services. A reasonably complete official statement comes in the DHSS evidence to the House of Commons Committee on Social Services (HC13 1984–85):

"– to enable an individual to remain in his own home wherever possible, rather than being cared for in a hospital or residential home;

– to give support and relief to informal carers (family, friends and neighbours) coping with the stress of caring for a dependent person;

– to deliver appropriate help, by the means which cause the least possible disruption to ordinary living;

– to relieve the stresses and strains contributing to or arising from physical or emotional disorder;

5

— to provide the most cost-effective package of services to meet the needs and wishes of those being helped;

— to integrate all the resources of a geographical area in order to support the individuals within it. The resources might include informal carers, NHS and personal social services and organised voluntary effort, but also sheltered housing, the local social security office, the church, local clubs, and so on."

3.7 This is a valuable approach, but needs to be supplemented. It makes no explicit mention of the need for assessment of the individual in his or her own situation, taking account of all the resources that may be available and the gap which may exist between the assistance those resources provide and the individual's needs. Nor is the potential for the preventative and rehabilitative value of community care made explicit. The recommendations propose that a more comprehensive statement should be drawn up to remedy these deficiencies.

Care and Support for Individuals

3.8 To translate broad community care objectives into action for individual people, those arranging public services must:—

i. have systems which enable them to identify those who have need of care and support in the community;

ii. assess those needs within the context of the individual's own situation;

iii. taking account of the views and wishes of the person to be cared for, and any informal carers, decide what packages of care would be best suited to the needs, whether provided directly or indirectly;

iv. determine the priority to be given to the case, given the total resources available and the competing needs of others;

v. arrange delivery of the services decided upon;

vi. keep under review the delivery of that package of services, and the individual's needs and circumstances.

Where services are provided directly those providing them will also have the usual line management responsibilities.

3.9 The first duty of identifying the people in need deserves extended comment. Systems to achieve this are essential because, by definition, those in need of care and support may not be able to obtain the information they need, or to act upon it, in order to inform the agencies concerned. Unless those charged with responsibility for meeting needs are reasonably sure that they have a good knowledge of the major needs in their area, and of the individuals who have those needs, they can have no assurance that their policies and actions focus the resources they manage on the individuals in greatest need.

Chapter 4: Responsibilities

4.1 This chapter deals with the question of responsibilities for community care.

4.2 I have found, along with most commentators on this subject, that there is at present insufficient clarity of responsibility for the arranging of publicly provided services in line with people's needs and service priorities. Where successes are achieved, they can as often as not be attributed to the flair and determination of individuals, in spite of the system rather than aided by it. It is unsafe to rely on this. It runs the risk that no-one is taking a sufficiently wide view of all the help that can be given, with the result that the most suitable forms of care are overlooked, priorities distorted and resources wasted. Also, present arrangements do not encourage systematic attempts to discover how helpful services are perceived to be by consumers, for example through market research techniques. The proposals are aimed at ensuring that, for community care, one authority is responsible for identifying and assessing needs, and organising suitable care.

Families and Informal Carers

4.3 The information provided to carers about service availability and how they might be helped with their onerous responsibilities is limited. A failure to give proper levels of support to informal carers not only reduces their own quality of life and that of the relative or friend they care for, but is also potentially inefficient as it can lead to less personally appropriate care being offered. Positive action is therefore needed to encourage the delivery of more flexible support, which take account of how best to support and maintain the role of the informal carer.

Voluntary Sector

4.4 The contribution of the voluntary sector could be developed further if the basis and management of funding were more appropriately applied. This is the subject of further comment in Chapter 8.

Private Sector

4.5 The contribution of the private sector is mainly in the field of residential care, but there has also been growth of private sheltered housing provision and, on a relatively small scale, organised domiciliary care services. The best examples show how services can respond very flexibly to meet the particular needs of individuals in a way that is acceptable to them and takes full account of their personal circumstances.

4.6 It is important that changes in the present systems for using public funds to support community care do not strengthen the potential monopoly power of the public sector and so restrict this contribution. There are similar dangers in the present system for regulation and inspection of residential and nursing homes, which can result in higher standards of provision being required from private (and voluntary) homes than similar homes in the public sector often provide. The proposals should encourage a proportionate increase in private and voluntary services, as distinct from directly provided public services. This process will aid consumer choice both by encouraging the development of a greater range of services and by increasing competition.

Social Services Authorities

4.7 Social services authorities[1] have the main local authority responsibility for community care. I have seen numerous examples of imaginative projects serving relatively small numbers of clients, and am aware of others, but have found in

---

[1] "Social services authority" throughout this report is used to refer to the responsibilities of the elected members of the local authority social services committee exercised through the officers of the social services department.

7

general that social services authority activities tend to be dominated by the direct management of services which take insufficient account of the varying needs of individuals.

4.8 There is only limited evidence of systematic planning to ensure that resources are targeted at the areas of greatest need. Without such planning, there is a danger that the concentration on child care duties and responsibilities (which are more explicitly stated in legislation and attract more political and public attention) may result in low priority being given to community care.

Housing Services   4.9 At present, housing authorities provide warden services in sheltered housing schemes and community alarm systems in addition to the "bricks and mortar" of the buildings themselves. Additionally, in shire districts the district authority is often responsible for the provision of a meals on wheels service. This dissipates responsibility for delivery of services and does not fit well with the changes in the overall role and function of housing authorities envisaged in the recent White Paper "Housing: the Government's Proposals" (Cm 214). In particular their role will change from one of concentrating on the direct provision of housing to concentrating on an enabling role. The recommendations go with the grain of these changes, and would confine housing authorities' responsibilities for community care to the provision of "bricks and mortar".

Other Local Authority Services   4.10 Education services can have a significant impact on community care for particular groups of individuals, especially handicapped children and mentally handicapped young people and adults. In general, there is little confusion of roles and responsibilities in this sphere. For other local authority services, there is minimal or even no need for specialist provision for consumers of community care, although service providers in such fields as leisure and recreational services and library services need to ensure that satisfactory arrangements exist for equal access and treatment.

Health Authorities   4.11 An individual's need for long term care and support may stem from a medical condition that itself requires medical treatment, whether regularly or occasionally. In addition, an individual's handicap or disability may affect their normal acute health care, e.g. a blind person may need some special arrangements for recognising different medicines which have been prescribed. The health care contribution to community care is to respond to both sets of need.

4.12 Acute hospital services and community care are complementary. There is, of course, interaction between them and in some cases there may be a need to improve planning and communication between different bodies, so that the appropriate range of services is readily available to patients when they are discharged from hospital. With this proviso, I believe that the assignment of responsibilities for acute health services is generally clear and the boundaries of responsibility are well defined.

4.13 It has been Government policy for many years that long stay hospitals for mentally ill, mentally handicapped and elderly people are not, in general, the right setting for people who do not need both medical supervision and nursing care to be available throughout twenty-four hours, although there will be a continuing need for some long stay hospital facilities. The recommendations are intended to enable that policy to be implemented more effectively.

4.14 Lack of clarity of responsibility has frustrated successful implementation to date. On the one hand, there is widespread concern that people have left long stay hospitals with inadequate care and support being provided in the community. On the other, we can see very full and elaborate support schemes being provided by health authorites, in preference to the less desirable conditions of long stay hospitals, although those schemes would not normally be thought of as health services. Equally, while there are successful joint community care projects linked to hospital closures, there is concern about the care and support available in the community for those who have never entered a long stay hospital, but who need a comparable level of care.

4.15 One particular problem, that of the transfer of employment for staff of former long stay hospitals, needs early resolution. The problem arises in cases where the support that staff used to provide in the hospital becomes the responsibility of the local authority, and in particular the social services department. Such issues must not be allowed to slow down the development of effective community care services, and I make recommendations about this in Chapter 7.

Family Practitioner Services

4.16 Primary health care services, including dental, opthalmic and pharmaceutical services make an important contribution to community care both in preventing the need for such care by health promotion, care and treatment, and by contributing when health care is one component of an individual's total needs. The general medical service, or family doctor service, is unique in having near universal contact with the whole population. I do not believe that the full potential of this contact has yet been realised. The present contract for general practitioners gives them a responsibility for "advice to enable them (patients) to take advantage of the local authority social services". Many general practitioners interpret this responsibility widely, and make sure that the social services authority is aware of their patients' major unmet (non-health) community care needs, but this is not universal. There is scope for action therefore to ensure that this useful role is fulfilled.

Financial Responsibilities

4.17 The ways in which money is spent on community care do not enable a comprehensive approach – to needs assessment, planning and delivery of services – to be achieved.

4.18 At the level of central government, large sums are provided through the health services, some of them earmarked for specific community care projects which may be linked to hospital closure programmes, and through social security, as supplementary benefit to eligible people in residential and nursing homes. None of central government's grant support for local authority expenditure is earmarked for community care.

4.19 At local government level, there may or may not be joint projects financed by health authorities; there will certainly be no responsibility for what is provided through social security.

4.20 The results are obvious and well documented. The system is almost designed to produce patchy performance: good where there happen to be earmarked funds and local goodwill and initiative; poor where, in spite of funds being available, the incentives to plan, prioritise, and organise across the whole field are negligible.

4.21 The separate funding of residential and nursing home care through social security, with no assessment of need, is a particularly pernicious split in responsibilities, and a fundamental obstacle to the creation of a comprehensive local approach to community care.

4.22 The demographic trends that already affect the demand for community care and will continue to do so over the coming decades are well known. As an example, between 1986 and 1996 the number of people aged over 85, who are most dependent on support from others, will grow by nearly 50 per cent. Thus the number of people of this age has risen from 459,000 in 1976 to 603,000 in 1986, and will rise to 894,000 by the year 1996. Also improvements in health and other care means that younger severely handicapped people are also surviving longer, with considerable care needs.

4.23 As well as demographic changes, future policy needs to be planned in the light of economic changes, in particular the significantly higher real incomes and greater wealth which today's middle-aged will have on reaching retirement. I discuss the opportunities for action in the light of this in Chapter 6.

Conclusions

4.24 There will always be multiple responsibilities for providing care, since people's needs, and the skills needed to meet them, are infinitely varied. The purpose of the recommendations is to create a system, underpinned by financial accountability, in which local responsibility for delivery of community care objectives is clear beyond doubt.

Chapter 5: Strategic Options

5.1 This chapter explains my approach to organisational, management and financial issues.

Organisation

5.2 One approach, which some advocate, would be to dispense with the present organisation and design new structures. I have not favoured this, partly because of the disruption and turbulence that would result to no real benefit, but mainly because I firmly believe that the major responsibility for community care rests best where it now lies: with local government. Elected local authorities are best placed, in my judgment, to assess local needs, set local priorities, and monitor local performance. What is needed is a strengthening and buttressing of their capacity to do this, by clarifying and where necessary adjusting responsibilities; and to hold them accountable.

5.3 I have not, therefore, favoured restructuring, whether by the creation of new elected or non-elected authorities, or major transfers of responsibility between existing authorities.

5.4 Nor have I seen advantage in seeking to construct a prescriptive approach to local organisations, for example by insisting that local management be divided by client groups. I see significant advantage in allowing local diversity and initiative.

5.5 The proposals will diminish the responsibility of social security for supporting residential and nursing home care, but to the advantage of community care services as a whole. Our social security system is essentially designed to provide a standard range of benefits for large numbers of people against objective tests of entitlement. It is not an appropriate system for the direct provision of individually tailored packages of support, within a finite community care programme. The proper contribution of the social security system to community care is to provide, for those who are eligible, a reliable source of income to meet normal living expenses and to help with housing expenses.

Management

5.6 I have no wish to be over-prescriptive about management. However, some things are fundamental, and in particular the creation of a budgetary approach, centrally and locally, which aligns responsibility for achieving objectives with control over the resources needed to achieve them, so that there is a built-in incentive and the facility to make the best use of the resources available. Such a system will facilitate effective planning and responsiveness to change. It is self-evident that resources must be consistent with the agreed responsibilities and objectives to be achieved within a given timescale. So, for example, if resources are not great enough to meet agreed objectives, a budgetary system will provide a firm information base from which to make decisions about either reducing the scale of set objectives or identifying the precise resources needed to discharge them. Such a system will also provide a spur to managers to provide themselves with better information, and to search for the most effective and efficient ways of meeting needs.

5.7 A similar approach is needed both at local and national levels to ensure that the entire resources allocated are properly identified and accounted for. The absence of such processes at national level is inconsistent with any claim that there are serious national policy objectives to be achieved. Such a system should be an integral part of the central decision-making and management process. Its purpose should be to ensure that:—

i.   national objectives and priorities are clearly established;

ii. the necessary resources (not just of money, but also people with the requisite skills and training) are available to enable the nationally set objectives and priorities to be translated into action;

iii. objectives and priorities for local action are established locally;

iv. central government has the necessary leverage to ensure that local objectives properly contribute to meeting national objectives;

v.   results are monitored locally so that there is local accountability for meeting local objectives and central accountability for meeting national objectives.

The recommendations provide a framework for the development of such a system.

Finance

5.8 The system of local political and managerial responsibility must be under-pinned by a suitable financial system. This is a keystone in the structure.

5.9 Under the present system of local government finance, local government raises its revenue from:—

- grant from central government in the form of either general block grant or specific grants for particular services or activities;

- local taxation in the form of domestic and non-domestic rates;

- fees and charges for services.

The percentage of expenditure supported by government grant has declined in the 1980s and this, combined with the increasing proportion of grant which goes to support specific activities, has reduced the block grant support for services such as community care.

5.10 The level of block grant which an authority gets is determined on an annual basis through the rate support grant settlement. Thus, unlike health authorities, local authorities do not have indicative figures for the grant that they can expect to receive in future years which would assist them to plan services for the years ahead. Moreover a complicated set of factors influence the amount of grant received by individual authorites and there can be considerable variation from year to year. Such uncertainty has been found to frustrate effective planning and is particularly serious where the plans of other statutory authorities (i.e. health authorities) are dependent upon steady progress being made. Social services authorities need security of funding if they are to plan to develop their community care services in a coherent way. Equally central government needs clear mechanisms to hold local authorities to account for centrally provided resources devoted to community care.

5.11 The new system of local government finance to be introduced in 1990 will:—

- replace domestic rates by the community charge;

- replace non-domestic rates by a uniform business rate;

- replace the block grant system by a new revenue support grant.

While the new system of central government grant is intended to be simpler than the existing system it will retain many of the features which have been found to impede the development of community care. The process of grant determination will still be an annual one and there is no proposal to issue indicative planning figures for future years.

5.12 For the purposes of this report, I have assumed that the new system of grant is unlikely to affect the delivery of community care objectives in any significant way. It follows that some additional change is needed to give central government the direct stake it should have in the delivery of its policies at local level. It needs to have that stake not just because of the intrinsic national importance of those policies, but also because of the considerable inter-relationships between what is done by local authorities, and what may or may not need to be done by others more directly accountable to central government, and in particular by health authorities.

5.13 On top of this, I am proposing switches of financial responsibility for community care to local authorities from both social security and health authorities. It is essential that the transferred funds reach their intended destination, i.e. local social services authorities, and do not end up in the general grant pool.

5.14 For all these reasons i.e.

- to recognise the interdependence of local and central government programmes;

- to provide a degree of central government influence and control;

- to create a more stable basis for planning and delivery of services; and

- to ensure transferred funds reach their intended destination,

I have recommended a programme of specific grants that is spelt out in more detail in the next chapter. That chapter also covers the way in which income from fees and charges should be taken into account.

Chapter 6: Recommendations

6.1 This chapter sets out the detailed recommendations for action.

RESPONSIBILITIES

**Local Authority
Social Services
Authorities**

6.2 Local authority social services authorities should be responsible for identifying people with community care needs in their area.

6.3 Where a social services authority has identified someone with community care needs, and that person has other needs e.g. for health care or housing, the authority should be responsible for ensuring that the other relevant public authorities consider whether, and if so what, they should do to contribute to the person's care and support.

6.4 Social services authorities should themselves be responsible for arranging for the needs of an individual for social, domestic and personal care and support to be assessed (and regularly re-assessed) in full consultation with the person concerned and any informal carers, so that these assessments take account of the individual's wider circumstances.

6.5 The social services authority must decide then what action to take itself. At the lowest level, support for informal care may be all that is needed. At the other extreme, multiple services may have to be arranged. It is recommended that social services authorities should develop and manage packages of care tailored to meet most effectively, within their budget and priorities, the needs of individuals.

6.6　In cases where a significant level of resources are involved a "care manager" should be nominated from within the social services authority's staff to oversee the assessment and re-assessment function and manage the resulting action. Where care is already being effectively managed, this proposal will amount to little more than making existing roles explicit.

6.7 Even when the situation is fairly stable, it is important that the individual and everyone else involved, including any informal carer, knows to whom to turn for immediate support. This might sensibly be the person with whom the individual has the most day-to-day contact. That person, regardless of their parent organisation, could be given responsibility for providing information to the social services authority about changes in the individual's circumstances that may affect the need for care and support.

6.8 Social services authorities should have sufficiently wide powers to enable them to provide goods and services to maintain or establish people, who might otherwise need to have institutional care, in their own homes. To that end, I propose that the community care element of the Social Fund should be withdrawn from the social security system and the funds earmarked for that purpose transferred to social services authorities. I do not recommend any extension of social services authorities' limited powers to make cash payments to individuals.

6.9 Social services authorities should:

i. ensure that information is readily available about community care and where and how to seek services that will contribute to that care. This should cover services provided by public authorities, the voluntary sector, and private businesses;

ii. develop and sustain informal and voluntary community care resources by supporting informal carers, volunteers, and voluntary organisations;

iii. maximise choice and competition by encouraging the further development of private services.

I deal below with control over standards.

Local Authority Housing Authorities, Housing Corporation

6.10 The responsibility of public housing authorities (local authority housing authorities, Housing Corporation etc.) should be limited to arranging and sometimes financing and managing the "bricks and mortar" of housing needed for community care purposes. Social services authorities should be responsible for arranging the provision of social, personal and domestic services in sheltered housing, and the finance for those services should be provided through social services, not housing budgets.

6.11 I do not intend this to prevent arrangements being agreed between housing authorities and social services departments, for example for the provision of wardens who carry out both property management and personal care responsibilities. Similar considerations in principle apply to alarm systems: the decision whether an alarm system would be an efficient means of meeting an individual's needs should be for the social services authority, which should also be responsible for financing those parts of a system that are not the landlord's fixtures and fittings.

Regional and District Health Authorities

6.12 The responsibilities of regional and district health authorities should in general continue to be the provision of health care. In broad terms this involves investigation, diagnosis, treatment and rehabilitation undertaken by a doctor or by other professional staff to whom a doctor (sometimes a general practitioner) has referred the patient. In addition, health authorities have important responsibilities for health promotion and the prevention of ill health. Health authorities should not provide services which fall outside this definition.

6.13 The community nursing services provided by the health authority are an important part of the health care contribution to community care. My recommendations on responsibilities may affect, but should in no way diminish, the contribution that community nursing makes to community care. Since my intention is to pinpoint responsibility for arranging the provision of services in the community, there is a great deal of room for flexibility over who does precisely what for whom, while – I hope – increasing the opportunities for making the best possible fit between needs and services provided and avoiding unnecessary duplication. In this way, the special skills of community nurses should be used to best effect.

Family Practitioner Services

6.14 The contract between the family practitioner committee and the general medical practitioner should be amended to specify that the GP, either directly or through his practice staff, should inform the social services authority of possible community care needs of any patients registered with him who seem to have such needs which are not being met and which appear to be unknown to the social services authority. The GP should also be able to satisfy himself that the social services authority has considered the case. The social services authority should therefore confirm that it has received the referral from the GP, and tell him what action it has decided to take.

Joint Planning and Action

6.15 The proposals mean that joint local planning and action will continue to be essential, but that responsibilities and accountability for the plans and action will be clearer than they are now. The framework for joint action should be determined locally. The existing joint consultative committees may provide a useful model, but the emphasis should be on the total management of community care services, not the delivery of a few special projects. Special attention should be given to services at the point of delivery, with the aim of putting into practice at that crucial point the proposals on the identification and assessment of need, consultation with carers and those being cared for, design of care packages, setting of priorities, and monitoring.

6.16 Social services authorities and health authorities should review each others' plans when they significantly affect community care. Where they interact, agreement on the action proposed on both sides is essential. In some cases the best way of achieving this will be through the preparation of a joint plan. Other agencies, and in particular the voluntary sector, will need to be involved, depending on the nature and scale of their contribution.

6.17 Authorities should have powers to enable them to undertake joint action, or to act as agents for each other. For example, a community nurse might check, on behalf of the social services authority, on the general well-being of one of her patients whose family are having difficulties supporting them at home. On a larger scale, the management of some existing facilities might be handled on an agency basis.

6.18 Such arrangements for joint planning and action do not in any way lessen the responsibility of individual agencies for their own functions and actions. But it must be emphasised that effective co-operation at the local level will be essential, both to the success of individual projects and, more broadly, if the whole range of community care services, is to be delivered effectively. The adequacy of arrangements for joint planning will therefore be a central area for scrutiny as part of the conditions of grant, which I discuss below.

Central Government

6.19 I recommend that there should be a Minister of State in DHSS, who is clearly identified as being responsible for community care. He should be supported by a designated group of senior officials including those with responsibilities for community care finance, community care policy, the operational distribution and monitoring of central government funds for community care, and the national inspection of standards of service provision. Experience of community care management, and familiarity with management of health services, should also be represented.

6.20 The Minister should promulgate a definition of community care values and objectives to guide its development. He should arrange for the distribution of central government funds to social services authorities, subject to the conditions I describe below.

6.21 The Minister would be responsible for ensuring that national policy objectives were consistent with the resources available to public authorities charged with meeting them and for monitoring progress towards their achievement.

FUNDING

Central Government

6.22 I recommend that community care needs, including the implications for revenue and capital, should be considered separately in the public expenditure planning process.

6.23 In order to provide the necessary basis for planning and implementation of the proposals, I recommend that central government should provide directly to social service authorities, by specific grant, a substantial proportion of the total public funds it estimates are needed to meet national objectives. This might be 50 per cent, or might be slightly lower (say 40 per cent–45 per cent) to indicate that the primary responsibility for community care should lie with local government.

6.24 The main component of the specific grant would be that part of the current rate support grant which is provided in respect of social services authority community care responsibilities. Additionally, provision would be transferred from the Social Fund to take account of the transfer of responsibilities recommended in paragraph 6.8.

6.25 The grant should be fixed as a proportion of the estimated total expenditure required. It should be distributed according to the best possible indicators of need, applied on an individual authority basis. Social services authorities would have discretion to "top up" from their other sources of funds.

6.26 A great deal of work will need to be done to develop satisfactory indicators of need. At the same time it is important that the formula should not be so complicated that it is difficult for either local authorities or people in general to understand its objectives. The mechanism for distributing grant should therefore as clearly and simply as possible reflect national policy objectives.

6.27 The basis of any formula should be the number of elderly, mentally handicapped, mentally ill and physically disabled people living within a local authority's boundaries. The number of people within other groups who need care are smaller, and the needs of the main four priority groups may be taken as a sufficient proxy for them. However the distribution formula should be kept under review to ensure that this is the case.

6.28 It is likely that a usable formula will depend on establishing "synthetic indicators" of need: correlations between such factors as age, and health, and the level of people's dependency on assistance.

6.29 These indicators would be the foundation of any distribution formula. Consideration should also be given, however, to the place of:

    i.   economic factors, such as levels of income and unemployment. The dependency indicators should reflect people's need for *publicly financed* care and support; in more wealthy areas more people will be able to buy care from both the private sector and social services authorities.

    ii.   the amount of private, voluntary and informal care in the area. This is also relevant to developing a picture of needs which the social services authority may have to arrange to meet.

    iii.   geographical disparities in the revenue and capital *costs* of arranging care, for example staffing costs in London.

6.30 In order to create the maximum possible assurance about future levels of funding, and facilitate sensible planning, changes in the relative proportion and distribution of grant should be kept to a minimum.

6.31 Within the overall specific grant structure, there should be provision for central government to make targeted specific grants available to social services authorities to facilitate transfers of responsibility. Such grants will be necessary in cases where projects are on a fairly large scale and have a high national priority, for example as part of a plan to develop community services and close a long-stay hospital. I discuss this particular case below.

6.32 In principle, funds intended for community care projects of the sort now funded through joint finance (i.e. money provided initially to health authorities) should in future go to local social services authorities.

6.33 Social services authorities already make charges for services directly provided, although practice varies widely. It seems right that those able to pay the full economic cost of community care services should be expected to do so. I therefore recommend that account should be taken in the distribution mechanism for general specific grant of the extent to which the local population are able to pay economic charges for services i.e. the actual care and support provided – not the assessment and other processes through which it is arranged.

Regional and District Health Authorities

6.34 I recommend that the contribution of regional and district health authorities to the delivery of community care objectives should be separately identified in their plans and budgets and ring-fenced. I do not believe that new funding mechanisms are needed.

PLANNING AND MANAGEMENT

6.35 As a condition for the payment of specific grant I recommend that social services authorities should prepare plans with costed objectives and timetables for implementation which demonstrate their approach to the delivery of community care in their areas, and the adequacy of their management systems. The plans should show that local activity has been well thought through in relation to local needs and that what is planned represents value for money. They should also give evidence of the support given to voluntary groups and their involvement in the preparation of the plan, as well as showing how informal carers are being supported. Importantly the plans should also demonstrate that systems for joint planning and action exist and that the other relevant agencies, particularly the health and housing authorities, are content with the proposals for action. Progress against past objectives should also be reported.

6.36 Responsibility for the detailed content of these plans will rest with local authorities, but central government should seek to establish, amongst other things, whether plans requiring joint action have been agreed with all concerned; and whether the role of social services authorities is being developed along the lines proposed. The Social Services Inspectorate will have a major part to play in this process.

SUPPORTING PEOPLE IN THE COMMUNITY INSTEAD OF IN LONG STAY HOSPITALS

6.37 The recommendations I have made above should provide a much better structure for the care and support of people who in the past would have been cared for in long stay hospitals, and for those who have already been discharged from such hospitals. I have in particular, recommended that a targeted specific grant should be available to social services authorities to enable them to build up services so that people can be discharged from long stay hospitals. Those services must include the nomination of a care manager for each long stay patient discharged. In parallel with this, specific plans should be made by regional health authorities for the reduction in long stay hospital beds and any necessary increase in the contribution of community health services to community care. Plans from the two agencies should be closely integrated and preferably be a single document. The need for the preparation of tightly drawn plans by both authorities should help to ensure that action is put in hand, without the need for fundamental restructuring at local level.

6.38 Central government should address the consequences of my proposals for capital expenditure by health and social services authorities. Closure of long stay hospitals will release capital assets. Providing necessary consequent services in the community will require some capital expenditure by local authorities.

PUBLIC FINANCE FOR RESIDENTIAL AND NURSING HOME CARE

6.39 I recommend that public finance for people who require either residential home care or non-acute nursing home care, whether that care is provided by the public sector or by private or voluntary organisations, should be provided in the same way. Public finance should only be provided following separate assessments of the financial means of the applicant (using a means test consistent with that for income support) and of the need for care. These assessments should be managed through social services authorities as follows.

6.40 The social services authority should establish a system, including arrangements for consultation when necessary with others, for enabling it to decide whether residential care (including what is now the care provided in non-acute nursing homes) is the most appropriate way of meeting care needs, in the light of the other options available. Depending on the individual's circumstances, consultation might include private or voluntary carers including informal carers, and health carers, as well, of course, as the person directly affected. The social services authority would take the final decision. In doing so, it would take into account all the information available from its own sources, and assessments of the individual's health care needs provided through the health authority and the relevant GP.

6.41 In some urgent cases decisions to provide residential care may have to be taken and implemented without full consultation. In those circumstances consultation should be arranged as soon as possible thereafter.

6.42 As part of the assessment process, the social security system should contribute an assessment of the financial means of the applicant, leading to a decision about whether there is an entitlement to an income related social security benefit (described hereafter as "residential allowance"). The rate of residential allowance should be set in the light of the average total of income support and housing benefit to which someone living other than in residential care would be entitled. It would be for the social services authority to pay the balance of the costs, if it concluded that residential care was the most appropriate way of meeting the individual's care needs.

6.43 When the financial assessment showed that there was no entitlement to the income related residential allowance, the information collected should enable the social services authority to decide how much of the total cost of the residential care should be charged to the individual.

6.44 Some people may seek residential care even though the social services authority cannot agree that their care needs justify such care. In those circumstances there should continue to be entitlement to the residential allowance, but no financial support should be given by social services authorities.

6.45 A decision is required about which social services authority should be responsible for financing care for an individual who moves between one authority's area and another's. I recommend that financial responsibility should be based on the individual's "ordinary residence". This is consistent with current social services legislation.

6.46 If the recommendations are accepted, transfer of resources between social security and specific grant for social services authorities will be needed to take account of the changed responsibilities. Equally a transfer in the opposite direction will be necessary to take account of the fact that residents of local authority provided residential care (commonly known as Part III) will be supported on the same basis as those in private and voluntary homes. The net effect will depend on the rate at which the social security residential allowance is set and will call for detailed assessment. "Public Support for Residential Care" (the report of a Joint Central and Local Government Working Party) provided useful illustrative calculations.

6.47 The pace of this transfer will depend on decisions about continuing support for existing residents both of private and voluntary homes and of Part III accommodation. It is important that the implementation of the changes proposed and the transfer of resources between agencies does not adversely affect the delivery of care to such individuals. Two approaches are possible: preservation of existing financial entitlements from the current funding agencies or preservation of the right to the existing form of care, but with responsibility for its management located clearly with the social services authority. If the latter is chosen, then a targeted specific grant, of the kind I recommend in paragraph 6.31, would be necessary to smooth the transition of responsibilities between the social security system and social services authorities, because of the wide variation between areas in the number of such recipients.

6.48 "Public Support for Residential Care" includes discussion (in Chapter 4) of other issues where changes in the current system might require decisions. These issues include respite care, day care, full time work, unregistered homes and personal expenses. I endorse the recommendations made on these issues.

THE PRIVATE CONTRIBUTION TO CARE

6.49 Social services authorities should not be allowed to become monopolistic suppliers of residential and non-acute nursing home care. Central monitoring of local plans and the distribution of grant should be used to prevent this, if necessary. Central government should not fund a general expansion of local authority run homes. The objective should be to encourage further development of the private and voluntary sectors.

6.50 The reorientation of social services authorities towards an enabling role will be particularly relevant here. They should seek to negotiate the best possible prices for individual places in residential and nursing home care, reflecting the particular care needs of the individuals concerned and local market conditions. They should look rigorously at the comparative costs of domiciliary services, where they may be judged sufficient and seek out the most efficient services there too, whether from the private, voluntary or statutory sectors.

6.51 The social services authority will have an important stake in the public financing of private and voluntary residential care. It will therefore need to consider whether, for instance, a significant input of domiciliary care, day care and help to use leisure time would be a better option, giving a better life for the individual, and making better use of public money. I stress that the outcome of assessment when residential care is being considered should not be a choice between residential care and very little else. Instead, residential care will be one means of providing care and support, with packages of other possibilities costing the social services authority nearly as much as residential care also being serious options. In time, this should transform the way in which community care is provided and viewed.

REGISTRATION AND INSPECTION

6.52 There is a continuing managerial responsibility for social services authorities in monitoring the standards of residential and domiciliary care services funded by them, whether provided directly or not. Formal arrangements for inspection and registration supplement, but do not replace, continuous management scrutiny and control.

6.53 I recommend that residential care and non-acute nursing home care should be subject to the same regime of regulation and inspection, which should be extended to cover small homes with less than four residents. Responsibility for regulation and inspection should rest with the social services authorities.

6.54 In discharging their responsibilities for the registration and inspection of residential homes and non-acute nursing homes, social services authorities should explicitly consider the arrangements for meeting the health care needs of residents, drawing on advice from the district health authority. These arrangements would be without prejudice to the responsibilities of health authorities and GPs for meeting the health care needs of their patients.

6.55 To help in the process of matching services with individuals' needs, each home should publish a statement of the services it provides. Different homes will seek to provide care to different types of residents, in some cases including the provision of respite care. It follows that a home should be registered in relation to its stated objectives for the residents it seeks to care for and what sort of care it seeks to provide.

6.56 The registration and inspection system should consider appropriate staffing as at least as important as other aspects of a home. In particular, the person in charge needs to have the skills, knowledge, experience and personal qualities to be able to create the necessary environment both for residents and staff so that the home can achieve its objectives. This will often include the recognition that the needs of residents may change over time, and that the objectives of the home and its staffing may need to change in order adequately to care for those residents who have made that home their own home.

6.57 Social services authorities should review the organisation and staffing of their registration and inspection units to ensure that they are suitable for carrying out these duties effectively.

6.58 I have already recommended that it should be a responsibility of central government to monitor the proper application by social services authorities of standards of registration and inspection, a task already being undertaken by the Social Services Inspectorate. Further decisions on statutory inspection will need to take account of the report of the working party chaired by Lady Wagner.

LONG TERM OPPORTUNITIES

6.59 In framing the recommendations, I have been conscious of the need to look ahead at possible future patterns of service provision, as well as at today's challenges. This final section therefore sets out the opportunities for early action to facilitate innovative developments in the future.

6.60 The majority of those who need care and support are elderly. In looking at future options for the funding of community care, planning needs to take account of the possibilities of individuals beginning to plan to meet their own care needs at an earlier stage in life. Recent changes in pension legislation have increased the opportunities available to employees to take more personal responsibility for planning their pension provision. Moves to make provision for anticipated community care needs is a logical extension of such an approach.

6.61 Many of the elderly have higher incomes and levels of savings in real terms than in the past. This trend will continue as the coverage of pension schemes grows. This growth in individually held resources could provide a contribution to meeting community care needs. Wider availability of information about the range of services would assist individuals in planning successfully for their own futures. This approach both encourages individual responsibility and assists consumer choice and may be a valuable way ahead. There are already a number of interesting schemes for encouraging owner occupiers to use their equity to provide income which can be used to pay for services in retirement and I believe that similar innovative schemes should be encouraged.

6.62 Encouraging those who can afford to plan ahead to do so should help to ensure that public resources are concentrated on those in greatest need.

6.63 I therefore recommend that central government should look in detail at a range of options for encouraging individuals to take responsibility for planning their future needs. This examination should include evaluating the potential of innovative service models, such as social maintenance organisations along the lines of the health maintenance organisations, which currently exist in the USA, and the incentives available through taxation and insurance systems for encouraging individual and corporate planning in this area, perhaps through the extension of occupational pension schemes.

Chapter 7: Implementation

Introduction
7.1 This chapter deals with implementation and some transitional issues, should the recommended scheme be accepted.

Central Government
7.2 The process of change should start with the designation of a Minister within the DHSS to be responsible for community care, and implementation of the agreed changes. This appointment should be at Minister of State level because of the scale of expenditure, the importance of the subject and the multiplicity of interests in what is to be done. I foresee two primary tasks: first, securing the necessary climate for implementation of the general approach and second, establishing and monitoring an implementation programme. These will be central to the work of the central implementation team, which should support the minister.

Legislation
7.3 New primary legislation will be required to implement several recommendations, in particular the transfer to local authorities of responsibility for providing public finance to support people in residential and non-acute nursing homes. Changes in and clarification of the responsibilities towards community care of social services authorities, health authorities, and general medical services are also likely to require primary legislation, as will the establishment of a specific grant system and the changes proposed to the responsibilities of the Social Fund and the existing joint planning and finance arrangements. Legislation should enable social services authorities to finance the provision of services by the private and voluntary sectors, as well as directly providing services. It should also facilitate joint action, where this is agreed locally.

7.4 Developing the implementation plan will require detailed specification of further tasks, with timetables and identification of the critical path towards implementation by a due date. Successful implementation will require a measure of general willingness to make the recommended processes work. The precise resource implications will need to be worked out in detail.

Objectives, Values and Information
7.5 There is a need for central government to make an early clear statement of the objectives and values underlying its community care policies, clarifying its view of the role of the public sector. It should also make general information available about access to public agencies providing community care. Detailed information should be provided locally, as I have recommended.

7.6 Central government has a responsibility for identifying and disseminating examples of good practice. This may be particularly important during the implementation period, as there is a danger of effort being wasted in the identification of identical solutions. This role should support rather than constrain the development of imaginative and entrepreneurial solutions at the local level.

Local Government
7.7 In shire counties, the local authorities with housing and social services responsibilities will not be identical. There will therefore need to be close co-operation if, for example, arrangements for the public finance and management of the warden services of sheltered housing are to work smoothly.

7.8 The recommendations, particularly the change in emphasis towards identifying suitable packages of care and the management disciplines associated with specific

23

grant, will increase the demands upon social services authorities' capacity for planning, budgeting, monitoring and other skills. Developing this capacity will be a considerable task for their management and leadership.

7.9 Ministers will need to consider what implications the recommendations have for child care services.

Health Authorities 7.10 The main effects on health authorities flow from the recommended clarification of their responsibilities. In particular, action will be needed to deal with the situation of some health authorities who have developed residential care and other non-acute services to meet functions which more appropriately will fall to be discharged by social services authorities. These services will need detailed scrutiny and action case by case. Various solutions are possible: for example, the health authority might agree to keep day-to-day management responsibility for a period after a formal transfer of financial responsibility and provision, but acting as an agent of the social services authority. A number of other models are possible. I emphasise the need for early action through the planning process in this area, rather than prescribing a model for every case.

Joint Planning and Action 7.11 I have emphasised the need for effective joint planning mechanisms at the local level. It is important that all authorities concerned review existing systems and make the necessary adjustments to them. In particular, new arrangements should concentrate on the whole spectrum of community care provision, rather than focusing too narrowly only on the needs of those discharged from long stay hospitals.

7.12 The Health Advisory Service, National Development Team for People with a Mental Handicap, and Social Services Inspectorate have provided assistance to authorities to develop realistic and workable joint plans and joint action. This sort of central activity will continue to make a valuable contribution locally.

Transfer of Staff from Health Authority to Local Authority Employment 7.13 It is important that the skills of staff formerly employed in long stay hospitals are not lost, as patients are discharged and responsibility for their care passes to another authority. Such staff are likely to have direct personal knowledge of individual former patients and their needs, as well as a wide range of skills which are equally valuable in a community care setting. There are legislative and other problems which inhibit the smooth transfer of staff between agencies at present, which can delay desirable changes.

7.14 There are a number of options for local action in regard to staff. They may be seconded to the local authority, which has the advantage of being a flexible approach. There can be locally arranged transfers to local authority employment with no redundancy compensation and with the retention of NHS superannuation scheme membership, which can be an important consideration for the staff concerned. Finally the health authority can make the staff redundant followed by engagement of the same staff by the local authority. Each of these options has its own advantages and disadvantages.

7.15 It is inexcusable for general progress to be halted because of this issue. I therefore recommend that central government make a clear decision on the action to be taken. If it is decided that the solution is not to involve legislation, this should be made clear to local management, who should also receive detailed guidance on which of the options are acceptable. It should then be a local responsibility to identify and implement the most suitable option for the individual case, taking account of the views expressed locally.

Chapter 8: Other Issues

Professional Roles 8.1 The proposals involve significant changes in role for a number of professional and occupational groups. In many cases their implementation will more sharply focus developments which are already taking place within professions. For example, many social services staff already have a managerial function, but my approach will give this added emphasis, for example in the development of the skills needed to buy in services. Other new skills, particularly in the design of successful management accounting systems and the effective use of the information produced by them, will be needed. The change in role of social services authorities might also allow them to make more productive use of the management abilities and experience of all their staff, including those who are not qualified social workers.

8.2 The recommendation in paragraph 6.14 implies a more systematic approach by all GPs to identifying the potential community care needs of their patients. The GP will have to consider all of his patients whose health status means they can be expected to have community care needs. The responsibility for arranging such systematic consideration will be the GP's, using the resources available to the practice in the most effective way.

8.3 The professional skills of community nurses and health visitors need to be effectively harnessed and their contribution in working with other professional groups fully recognised. In particular, the supportive skills and the ability to develop independence currently displayed by community psychiatric nurses and registered mental handicap nurses have an invaluable role to play in meeting the needs of both clients and informal carers.

8.4 The Audit Commission recommended the creation of a new occupation of "community carers" to undertake the front line personal and social support of dependent people. This might be a development of the roles of some home helps/home care assistants, community nursing assistants and residential care staff. There is scope for the development of multi-purpose domiciliary services along these lines by social services authorities, the voluntary sector and the private caring organisations. If this is acted upon, it will be vital to ensure that job descriptions enable individual workers to provide the assistance required without demarcation problems arising. The management of and support for such staff groups will need to be carefully planned.

Training 8.5 Ensuring that staff have the necessary skills to discharge their functions is a key task for any organisation, particularly one which is undergoing a significant degree of change. It will therefore be essential that the training implications of the recommendations are kept in mind throughout the implementation period. I recommend, as a first step, that central government should make a full assessment of the training implications of the proposals for all groups concerned. This section highlights some particular areas for attention.

8.6 Recruitment and in-service training systems for professional social services staff at both the national and local level will need to give greater emphasis to management skills to reflect the proposed change in emphasis of social services authorities' role. The same is true of qualifying training for social workers. A further aspect of training of particular relevance to social services authorities is the transfer of skills from professional staff to informal carers. Staff need to be trained to regard such support and training as an essential part of their job, and have the knowledge and skills to undertake the work effectively.

8.7 The training needs of the "community carers" mentioned in paragraph 8.4 also need to be defined. Action in this area should take account of the useful initiatives currently being pursued by the National Council for Vocational Qualifications involving the Central Council for Education and Training in Social Work, the United Kingdom Central Council, the Local Government Training Board and others.

8.8 Staff need training to fulfil their own roles, but also need to understand the contribution of other professions to community care. Insularity among individual professional groups can lead to failures of communication and inability to recognise both needs and options for meeting them. The need for effective collaboration in training matters at the local level to tackle this should be addressed by all authorities, both during the implementation period and as an ongoing task.

Multi-Racial Society

8.9 Both policy and action need to respond to the multi-racial nature of British society. The emphasis on the responsibility of the social services authority to assess need, and arrange appropriate packages of services for individuals *within their own situations*, should help to ensure that the different needs of people with different cultural backgrounds are properly considered. All staff involved will need to be trained to develop the appropriate knowledge and skill to do this successfully.

Voluntary Sector

8.10 To develop the potential contribution of the voluntary sector further, financial support for its role needs to be provided on a clearer basis, fully understood by all concerned. I therefore see a need for clear agreements to be made between public agencies and not-for-profit bodies on the basis of public agency funding. This may be, for example, on a fee per client basis, or a contract providing that the not-for-profit body should provide a given level of service. In either case, this should allow the social services authority to hold the not-for-profit body to account for the proper use of public funds. Equally, to allow voluntary bodies a greater degree of certainty in their planning, a reasonable degree of notice should be given before the basis of funding is changed, and public agencies must recognise that short-term project grants are not an appropriate way of providing reliable funding for ongoing work.

8.11 In addition to the direct provision of services, the voluntary sector fulfils a variety of other roles, including those of:—

- self-help support group
- information source/source of expertise
- befriending agency
- advocate for individuals
- constructive critic of service providers
- public educator
- pilot of new approaches to services
- campaigner.

All or a substantial number of these roles may often be combined in one small organisation. As these can be vital in helping to make the best use of public funds, they may often merit some public financial support. This is probably best provided as a general core grant to the voluntary organisation, from the social services authority at the local level, or from DHSS for national organisations. Informal support, for example by way of advice, will also be valuable.

Conclusion

Implementation of the proposals will increase the ability of managers in all community care services to ensure that:

- the right services are provided in good time, to the people who need them most;

- the people receiving help will have a greater say in what is done to help them, and a wider choice;

- people are helped to stay in their own homes for as long as possible, or in as near a domestic environment as possible, so that residential, nursing home and hospital care is reserved for those whose needs cannot be met in any other way.

These are the ends to be obtained. If the proposals themselves concentrate on means, that is because I was asked to look at systems and found that the blockages to progress lie there.

Ensuring that for each locality someone, at both the political and managerial levels, is charged with delivering community care policies *and* is given control of the necessary resources will help both to create new opportunities to improve the quality of services available and to obtain better value for money from them. What up to now has been exceptional progress, in spite of the obstacles, should become the norm.

Merely to tinker with the present system would not address the central issues and would forego the benefits that could be obtained from more concentrated action. The opportunity exists to create a partnership in the delivery of care – between central and local government; between health and social services; between government and the private and voluntary sectors; between professionals and individuals – to the benefit of those in need. The proposals as a whole – and no single one on its own – are aimed at enabling that opportunity to be taken.

Printed in the United Kingdom by Her Majesty's Stationery Office

Dd 292326 C50 1 90 19585